AF228331

Searchlight Books™

World Traveler

Travel to Morocco

Matt Doeden

Lerner Publications ◆ Minneapolis

Content consultant: Carla Joubert, Associate Professor, African and World History, Joliet Junior College

Lerner Publications Company
An imprint of Lerner Publishing Group, Inc.
241 First Avenue North
Minneapolis, MN 55401 USA

For reading levels and more information, look up this title at www.lernerbooks.com.

Main body text set in Adrianna Regular.
Typeface provided by Chank.

Map illustration on page 29 by Laura K. Westlund.

Photo Editor: Annie Zheng

Library of Congress Cataloging-in-Publication Data

Names: Doeden, Matt, author.
Title: Travel to Morocco / Matt Doeden.
Description: Minneapolis : Lerner Publications, [2023] | Series: Searchlight books : world traveler | Includes bibliographical references and index. | Audience: Ages 8–11 | Audience: Grades 4–6 | Summary: "With borders on the Atlantic Ocean, the Mediterranean Sea, and the Sahara Desert, Morocco has been an important part of African and European history. Discover Morocco's rich culture and history since gaining independence in 1956"— Provided by publisher.
Identifiers: LCCN 2022011877 (print) | LCCN 2022011878 (ebook) | ISBN 9781728457864 (lib. bdg.) | ISBN 9781728463988 (pbk.) | ISBN 9781728461960 (eb pdf)
Subjects: LCSH: Morocco—Juvenile literature.
Classification: LCC DT305 .D64 2023 (print) | LCC DT305 (ebook) | DDC 964—dc23/eng/20220415

LC record available at https://lccn.loc.gov/2022011877
LC ebook record available at https://lccn.loc.gov/2022011878

Manufactured in the United States of America
1-50814-50153-7/5/2022

Table of Contents

Chapter 1

GEOGRAPHY AND CLIMATE

Morocco is a country of contrast. From the shores of the Atlantic Ocean to the sands of the Sahara Desert, Morocco holds a vibrant landscape, culture, and history. Morocco is in northwest Africa. It borders the Atlantic Ocean to the east and the Mediterranean Sea to the north. Algeria lies to the west, while Morocco's disputed Western Sahara region lies to the south. Past this southern region lies Mauritania.

The Land

Morocco has three main regions: coastal lowlands, interior highlands, and the Sahara Desert. The coastal lowlands hug the shores of the Atlantic Ocean and Mediterranean Sea. This land is good for farming and is home to most of Morocco's people.

Farther inland, the land rises into mountain ranges and high plateaus. The Rif Mountains lie in the north. The Atlas Mountains in central Morocco include Toubkal, the country's highest peak at 13,665 feet (4,165 m) above sea level. The Sahara Desert covers southern Morocco.

The Atlas Mountains rise in southern Morocco and stretch northeast all the way to Tunisia. They are home to the Berber people.

The Draa River crosses the desert in southern Morocco. The river starts in the Atlas Mountains.

Rivers and Lakes

Morocco is mostly dry in the south. But many rivers flow out of the mountains. The Draa is Morocco's longest river. It flows 680 miles (1,100 km) from the Atlas Mountains to the Atlantic Ocean. Moroccans rely on it for drinking water and for irrigating their crops. Parts of the Draa run dry each year. The Oum Er-Rbia River is in the west, and the Moulouya and Sebou Rivers are in the north.

AL WAHDA DAM RESERVOIR LAKE

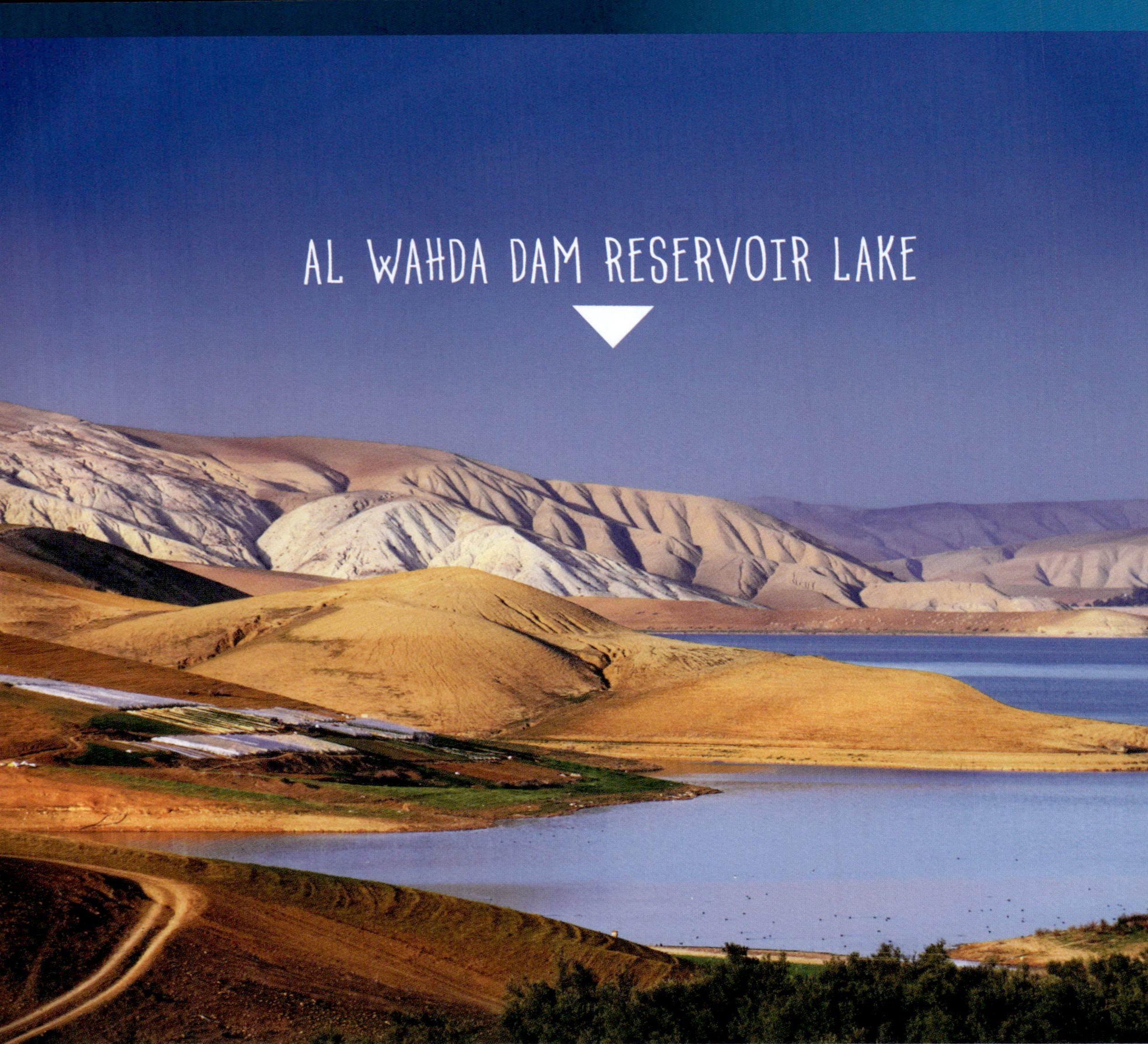

The largest natural lake in Morocco is Tislit Lake.
Like many of Morocco's lakes, it lies high in the Atlas
Mountains. Tislit Lake covers 1.2 square miles (3.1 sq. km).
The Al Wahda Dam on the Ouergha River is the largest
dam in Morocco and the second largest in Africa.

People can see the beauty of the Atlas Mountains at Toubkal National Park in central Morocco. Hikers, climbers, and nature lovers won't want to miss it! A trip to the summit of Toubkal is the highlight of any visit. But pack plenty of water and snacks. The trail to the top takes five to seven hours to hike!

Climate

Morocco has many climates. Northern Morocco has a Mediterranean climate. This climate has hot, dry summers and mild, wet winters. In Morocco's highlands, temperatures are colder and rainfall higher. Snow even falls in the higher parts of the Atlas Mountains.

To the south and east of the Atlas Mountains lies an arid climate. It's hot year-round, and little rain falls. In spring and summer, a wind called the sharqī blows hot, dusty air over other parts of southern and central Morocco.

Chapter 2

HISTORY AND GOVERNMENT

Scientists found human fossils in Morocco that date back 315,000 years. Some of Morocco's earliest people belonged to the Aterian culture. They made stone tools and were one of the first cultures to use bows and arrows. A group called the Berber people have lived in North Africa from at least 3000 BCE. They now live in small groups with no large government.

Starting around 1200 BCE, many civilizations rose and fell in this area. The Phoenicians invaded and built

The ancient city of Lixus was built by the Phoenicians sometime between 800 and 600 BCE. Later, Rome took over the city after conquering the Carthaginian Empire.

colonies on the coast. The Phoenicians were a people who traded and built cities all around the Mediterranean. A thousand years later, the area was taken as part of the Carthaginian Empire. Next, the Roman Empire took it.

The Umayyad Caliphate conquered in the 600s and introduced Islam and the Arabic language to the region. In the 700s, the Idrīsid dynasty took control of northern Africa and founded the city of Fez as their capital.

European Control and Independence

In the 1800s, European countries began taking control of parts of Morocco. Spain, France, and Portugal all held power at times. European colonists flocked to Morocco, taking land and resources from the native peoples who lived there.

Native Moroccans began to rise up against these foreign powers. Starting in 1921, Abd el-Krim, a political and military leader, led revolts in the Rif Mountains. The fighting lasted five years until Spanish and French forces ended it.

In 1907, some Moroccans attacked a French train because it ran over sacred land. In response, France attacked the city of Casablanca with battleships.

During the Rif War, Spanish troops took part in the first sea landing to use tanks and aircraft.

After France sent away Morocco's leader, Sultan Mohammed V, many people protested. When France let Mohammed V come back to Morocco, he fought for independence. Morocco gained independence in 1956. One year later, Sultan Mohammed V became the first king of independent Morocco.

Toward Democracy

Independence was sometimes difficult for Morocco. The new nation tried to give its people some democratic power. But kings often tried to take that power away. Morocco and Algeria also fought over control of the Western Sahara. This war cost many lives and a lot of money, and Western Sahara remains disputed territory.

Life in Morocco became much better in the 1990s. In 1999, Mohammed VI became king. Many Moroccans protested for greater democracy. Because of this, Mohammed VI changed Morocco's government to give more power to the people.

Thousands of Moroccans gathered in a demonstration for women's rights in Rabat, Morocco, on March 12, 2000.

Let's Celebrate:
Independence Day

Morocco's Independence Day is November 18, the day that King Mohammed returned to Morocco. French-speaking Moroccans know it as Fête de l'Indépendance. People celebrate with parades that honor the fight to gain freedom from European control. They eat traditional Moroccan foods such as lamb kabobs, sing the national anthem, and fly the country's flag.

The Moroccan parliament building is located in the capital city of Rabat.

Government

Morocco's government is a constitutional monarchy. A monarch is the head of the government. But Morocco's constitution limits the monarch's powers.

The government has three branches. The legislative branch passes the country's laws. It's made up of the Assembly of Representatives of Morocco and the Assembly of Councilors. Moroccans vote for their representatives in these lawmaking bodies.

The prime minister oversees the executive branch. It enforces laws. The judicial branch applies the law. The Supreme Court is the highest court in Morocco. The monarch appoints judges to the Supreme Court.

Chapter 3

CULTURE AND PEOPLE

Many different people call Morocco home. About 66 percent of Moroccans identify as Arabs. They descend from people who lived on the Arabian Peninsula. About 33 percent of Moroccans identify as Berbers. They descend from people who have lived in North Africa for tens of thousands of years. Other Moroccans come from a range of ethnic backgrounds, including some of Jewish descent.

Religion

About 99 percent of Moroccans are Muslims. They follow
the Islamic faith. Islam is the official state religion of Morocco.
The rest of Morocco's people are Christian, Jewish, or follow
the Bahá'í Faith. Many Jewish people lived in Morocco. But
centuries-long conflict between Jews and Muslims have driven
most of them out of the country. These days there are only
about twenty-five hundred Moroccan Jews.

Let's Celebrate:
Marrakech Biennale

Every two years the city of Marrakech celebrates modern artists of all kinds at the Marrakech Biennale. Artists from all over Morocco and even around the world come to the city to show their work and support one another. Thousands of visitors travel to Marrakech to watch movies, meet authors, and see art by new artists.

Many signs in Morocco are written in two languages.

Language and Writing

Morocco has two official languages, Arabic and Berber. Arabic is the most commonly spoken. Moroccans speak Darija, a dialect of Arabic. Several dialects of Berber also exist. The official dialect in Morocco is Tamazight. French is also used in Morocco for business and government.

While some Moroccans write in Darija, most use Modern Standard Arabic (MSA). MSA is the form of Arabic used worldwide. It appears in most Islamic religious texts. Arabic letters are formed from right to left instead of left to right. Some Moroccans also use Latin letters, like those used in English, to form Arabic words, especially in electronic communication.

Food and Art

African, Arabian, and European cultures have influenced Morocco. So it's no surprise that its people enjoy a wide range of foods. But many Moroccan dishes have one thing in common. They're spicy! Moroccan cooks use saffron, turmeric, ginger, cumin, and other spices to give their food a flavorful kick.

One of Morocco's most famous dishes is couscous. These small grains of rolled wheat are boiled like pasta. Couscous is served with meats such as chicken, beef, and lamb. Moroccans also use vegetables like potatoes, onions, carrots, and zucchini.

Step into a building that once served as home to the sultans of Morocco. The Dar al-Makhzen in the city of Tangier is a building made for a king. Visitors can visit the Museum of Moroccan Arts and Antiquities inside. The museum has works of art and artifacts that teach about Morocco's rich history.

TRADITIONAL WOVEN CARPETS

Moroccan art often features bright, vibrant colors. The country is famous for rugs and carpets that are handmade using methods handed down from generation to generation. Moroccan craftspeople also create beautiful jewelry, pottery, leather goods, and more.

Chapter 4

DAILY LIFE

More than 36 million people live in Morocco. Over half of all Moroccans live in urban areas. Casablanca is Morocco's largest city. It has 3.8 million people. Other big cities include Fez, Tangier, Marrakech, and the capital, Rabat. Many Moroccans work in manufacturing and tourism. Moroccans in rural areas often work in agriculture. They grow crops such as citrus fruits, grains, olives, and dates.

All Moroccan children between the ages of six and fifteen are supposed to attend school. But not all of them do, especially in rural areas.

The Future

Morocco is a growing country. But it faces a lot of challenges. Many of Morocco's rural people don't have access to the same services that urban Moroccans have. Their education rates are lower. They have less access to health care. And they often have lower incomes.

Climate change is another concern for Moroccans. Experts believe climate change could cause droughts.

Moroccans grow olives, grapes, and oranges on the coast. Climate change might make it harder to get enough water to grow these foods.

This could make it hard to grow food. Coastal areas could be flooded by rising sea levels. But Moroccans are taking an active role in slowing down climate change. In 2019, it built the world's largest concentrated solar farm to produce clean electricity. Moroccans hope that with time, they can overcome the challenges they face and make Morocco an even stronger country.

Map and Key Facts

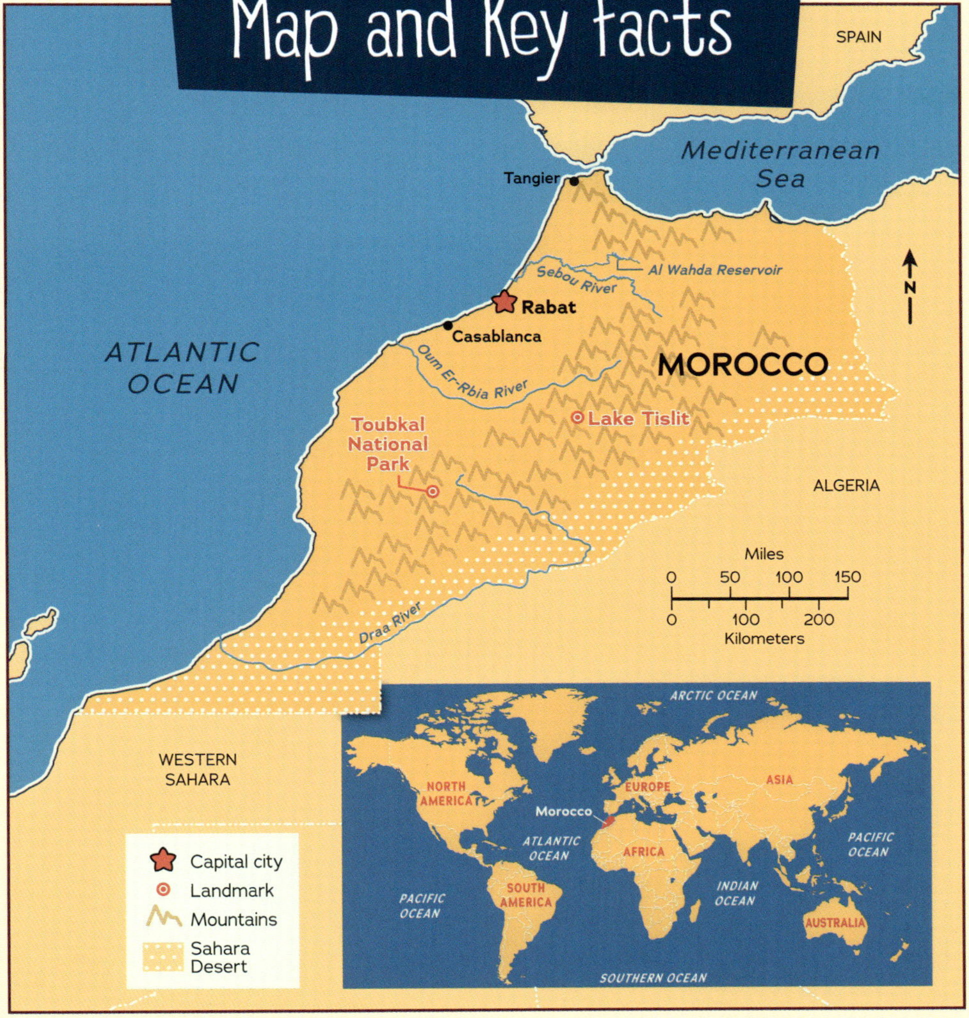

Flag of Morocco

- **Continent: Africa**
- **Capital city: Rabat**
- **Population: 35.5 million**
- **Languages: Arabic, Berber, and French**

Glossary

arid: receiving very little rain

dialect: a form of a language spoken in a certain region or by a certain group

dispute: to question or fight over

drought: a long period with very little or no rain

income: a gain usually in money that comes in from labor, business, or property

legislative: the lawmaking branch of government

monarch: a person that rules over a kingdom or empire, such as a king, queen, or emperor

plateau: a region of high, mostly level ground

sharqī: a hot, dry, dusty wind that blows out of the Sahara

sultan: an Islamic ruler

Learn More

Drummond, Allan. *Solar Story: How One Community Lives alongside the World's Biggest Solar Plant.* New York: Farrar Straus and Giroux Books for Young Readers, 2020.

Facts about Morocco
https://www.kids-world-travel-guide.com/morocco-facts.html

Koontz, Robin. *Learning about Africa.* Minneapolis: Lerner Publications, 2016.

Morocco Facts for Kids
https://kids.kiddle.co/Morocco

National Geographic Kids: Morocco
https://kids.nationalgeographic.com/geography/countries/article/morocco

Perritano, John. *Morocco.* New York: AV2 by Weigl, 2019.

Index

Photo Acknowledgments

Image credits: Abril Campana/Shutterstock, p. 5; Ikpro/Shutterstock, p. 6; Eric Valenne geostory/Shutterstock, p. 7; Natalia Davidovich/Shutterstock, p. 8; Ibrahim Oubahmane/ Shutterstock, p. 9; Pavliha/Getty Images, p. 10; K.M. Westermann/Getty Images, p. 12; Scherl/ Süddeutsche Zeitung Photo/Alamy Stock Photo, p. 13; Photo12 Collection/Alamy Stock Photo, p. 14; Driss Benyatouille/Gamma-Rapho/Getty Images, p. 15; AP Photo/Jalil Bounhar, p. 16; Hamza Makhchoune/Shutterstock, p. 17; Pete Niesen/Shutterstock, p. 19; REUTERS/Youssef Boudlal/Alamy Stock Photo, p. 20; jsorde/Shutterstock, p. 21; Sebastian Condrea/Getty Images, p. 22; Color Chaser/Shutterstock, p. 23; Yelo Jura/Shutterstock, p. 24; Mustapha GUNNOUNI/Shutterstock, p. 26; encrier/Getty Images, p. 27; Japhotos/Alamy Stock Photo, p. 28; Laura Westlund/Independent Picture Service, p. 29.

Cover: Eloi_Omella/Getty Images.